# Jackie Robinson

SADDLEBACK
EDUCATIONAL PUBLISHING

# Saddleback's Graphic Biographies

ISBN-13: 978-1-59905-225-0
eBook: 978-1-60291-588-6

Printed in Malaysia

22 21 20 19 18   9 10 11 12 13

## JACKIE ROBINSON

The year was 1947. In Ebbets Field in Brooklyn, one black man stood alone at first base—the first African American ever to play baseball in the major leagues.

IN HIS TEN YEARS
WITH THE BROOKLYN DODGERS,
JACKIE ROBINSON
BROKE THE COLOR BARRIER
AND CHANGED
THE SPORTS WORLD.

Jack Roosevelt Robinson was born in a sharecropper's cabin in Georgia on January 31, 1919.

He's a fine boy, Mallie!

Bless him! I just pray he has a chance to make something of his life!

A few months later, Jackie's father disappeared.

He's just run away and left his family behind. I don't know where he is!

I don't believe it! I think you do know!

Get out of my house and off my land! I'll keep your share of the crop for damages!

Sad and angry, Mallie Robinson moved her family away, with no pay for the past year's work.

A few months later ...

How would you like to move to California? My brother Burton writes that it's like the Promised Land!

They left Georgia in May 1920.

Here it comes, children, the freedom train!

But in Pasadena, California, things were not much better at first.

Now children, mind your aunt while I go out to find a job.

I can't find this address. I'll ask in here.

WELFARE
DISTRICT

ONE WAY

I wonder if you could help me.

That's what we are here for!

INFORMATION

A little later, Mrs. Robinson returned home.

Mallie! I didn't know you in those clothes!

Welfare gave them to me— and clothes for the children, too!

Best of all they gave me a grocery order. And money to help with the rent! And I got a job!

Later, Mrs. Robinson's sister died.

Willa Mae, I have to work. There's no one to look after Jackie. You'll have to take him to school with you.

But at school ...

But Willa Mae, you can't bring your brother to school! He's too little! He can't even talk!

The next day, Mrs. Robinson went to school with the children.

I'd rather work than ask welfare for more money. But I can't work if I have to stay home with Jackie!

Could Willa Mae just leave Jackie in the sandbox everyday? He's a good boy. He won't bother anybody!

All right Mrs. Robinson, go to work and don't worry. We'll look after Jackie.

Thank you!

So Jackie spent his first school year in the sandbox.

Willa Mae, there's a storm coming. Bring Jackie inside!

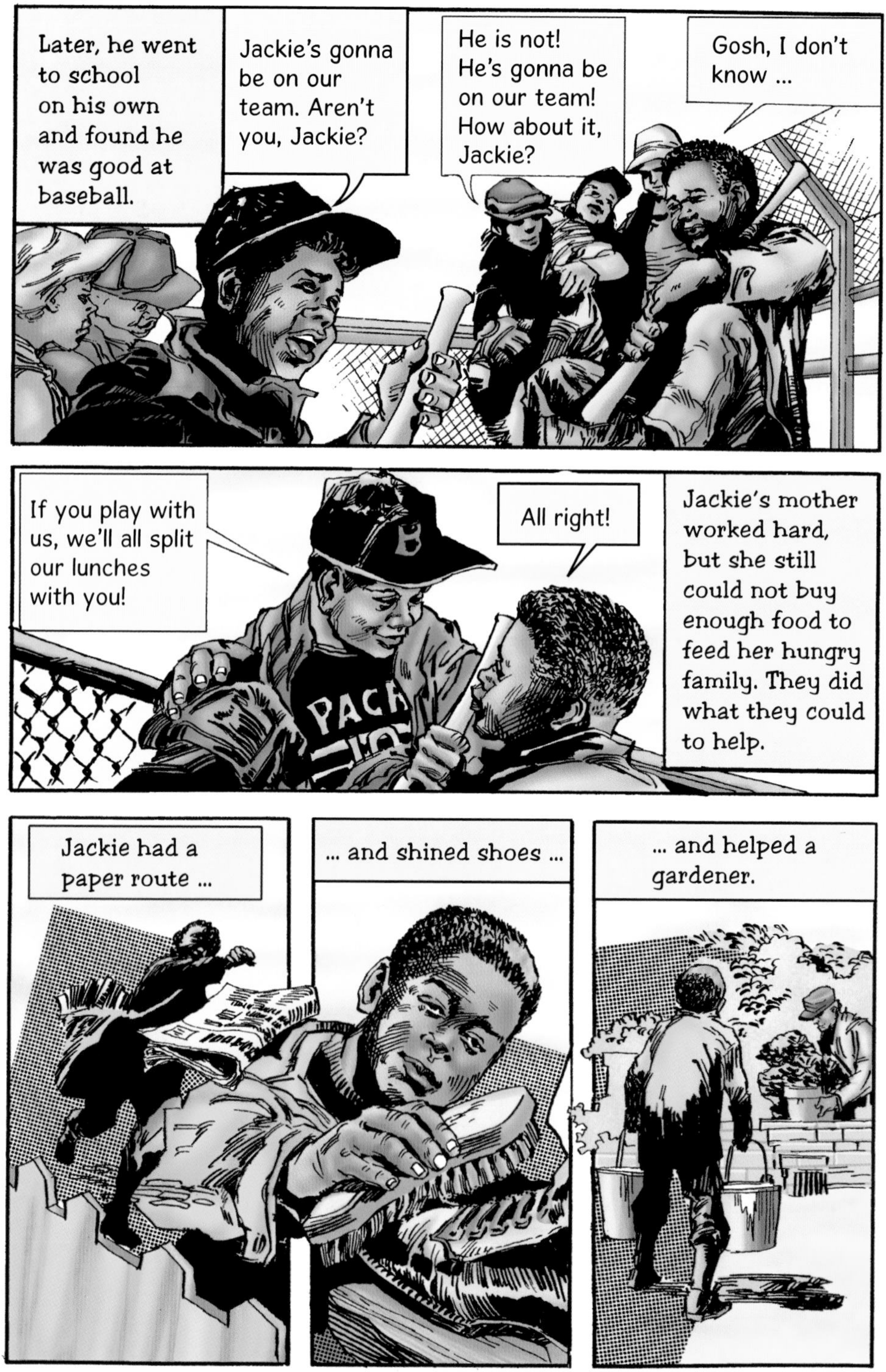
Later, he went to school on his own and found he was good at baseball.
Jackie's gonna be on our team. Aren't you, Jackie?
He is not! He's gonna be on our team! How about it, Jackie?
Gosh, I don't know ...
If you play with us, we'll all split our lunches with you!
All right!
Jackie's mother worked hard, but she still could not buy enough food to feed her hungry family. They did what they could to help.
Jackie had a paper route ...
... and shined shoes ...
... and helped a gardener.

And on payday ...

Mama! Mama! I've got a dollar for you!

Thank you, son. You know every dollar helps! But I want you to save enough money so you can go through school.

But he did not work all the time.

Hey, man, we're the Pepper Street Gang. You wanna join?

Sure! What do you do?

Swipe golf balls, throw mud at cars, anything we can think of!

The gang had trouble with the police.

Look at that! Mud all over my windshield.

You kids will wind up in reform school if you don't watch out!

But in high school, Jackie found a better way to spend his time.

When he graduated in 1937, he had won a letter in each of four sports.

He won athletic scholarships to pay his expenses to Pasadena Junior College and then to the University of California, Los Angeles.

Yaaaaaaaaaaay, Robinson!

Again at UCLA, he won a letter in four sports—the first student to ever do so.

Also, he met a young lady.

Rae, I want you to meet Jackie Robinson. Jackie, this is Rachel Isum.

Soon they were great friends.

It's funny ... I can tell you anything and you understand it, even if you disagree!

And it's funny, but before I met you, I thought you were just a stuck-up football player!

Then, before he finished his last college year, Jackie was offered a job.

But Jackie, you should finish college and get your degree.

It is the kind of job that I want working with young people. And I want to help you. You've been working hard ever since I can remember!

But in a few months, World War II broke out in Europe. Jackie's government job was cancelled.

You're a great athlete. Can't you get a job as a professional?

No major football, baseball, or basketball clubs hire black players! But I have been offered a job with the Honolulu Bears.

He went to Honolulu. On weekends he played football with the Bears.

During the week he worked at a construction job near Pearl Harbor.

What are these things we're building?

Ammunition shelters. Guess they're expecting trouble.

The football season ended. On December 5, 1941, Jackie sailed for home. Two days later ...

The Japanese have bombed Pearl Harbor, and the United States is at war! We hope to reach port safely, but we are passing out life jackets.

At home again, Jackie was soon in the army. He went to officer's training school and became a lieutenant.

Lieutenant Robinson, report to the 761st Tank Battalion at Fort Hood, Texas.

Yes, sir!

At Fort Hood, he was put in charge of a tank platoon.

Sergeant, I don't know anything about tanks. You and the men do! I'll count on you and ask questions and try to learn.

Yes, sir!

The men did not expect a lieutenant to admit he didn't know. They worked hard for Jackie.

A few weeks later ...

Lieutenant, your platoon has one of the best records in the unit. I'm giving you a special commendation.

Thank you, sir! But I arrived here knowing nothing about tanks!

Any praise goes to the sergeant and men. They did the work, and taught me, too!

However you did it, Lieutenant. You showed leadership and got results!

One day Jackie took a bus on the army post.

Hey, you! You can't sit there. Move to the back!

Are you talking to me?

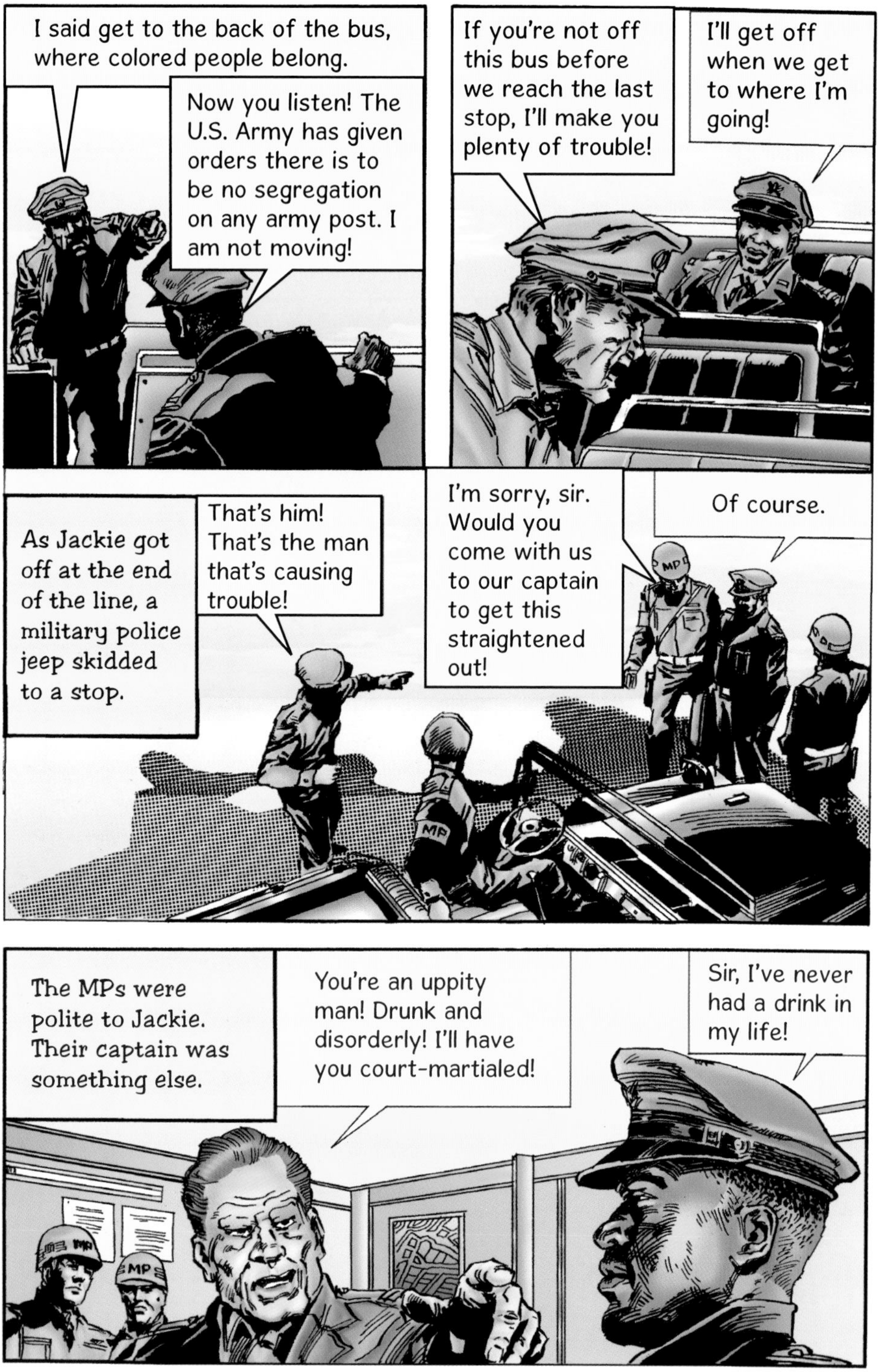
I said get to the back of the bus, where colored people belong.
Now you listen! The U.S. Army has given orders there is to be no segregation on any army post. I am not moving!
If you're not off this bus before we reach the last stop, I'll make you plenty of trouble!
I'll get off when we get to where I'm going!
As Jackie got off at the end of the line, a military police jeep skidded to a stop.
That's him! That's the man that's causing trouble!
I'm sorry, sir. Would you come with us to our captain to get this straightened out!
Of course.
The MPs were polite to Jackie. Their captain was something else.
You're an uppity man! Drunk and disorderly! I'll have you court-martialed!
Sir, I've never had a drink in my life!

Later, Jackie's colonel sent for him.

They've made charges. There will be a court-martial, but I intend to see that any man in my outfit, black or white, is treated fairly!

That's all I ask, sir.

Other black officers backed Jackie.

We'll see that the country knows what's happening. We're writing to the newspapers.

And to the National Association for the Advancement of Colored People!

And at the trial ...

We find Lieutenant Robinson *not guilty* of all charges.

Soon after, Jackie was discharged from the army. He hurried home.

I have a job playing baseball with a black team, the Kansas City Monarchs. Let's get married!

Soon, Jackie. But let's see how it turns out.

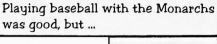

Playing baseball with the Monarchs was good, but ...

Seems like we spend all our time riding buses.

All night and playing baseball all day. I don't know how long I can stand it!

The food was bad, too.

Greasy hamburgers and cold coffee. We never have a decent meal!

Yeah! They'll sell food to blacks— as long as we take it outside to eat it!

I want to make some money, get married, and help my mother. But how? There's just no future for an African American athlete in this Jim Crow world!

And then ...

Look, Robinson, Branch Rickey, the boss of the Brooklyn Dodgers, wants to start a new league for black players.

So?

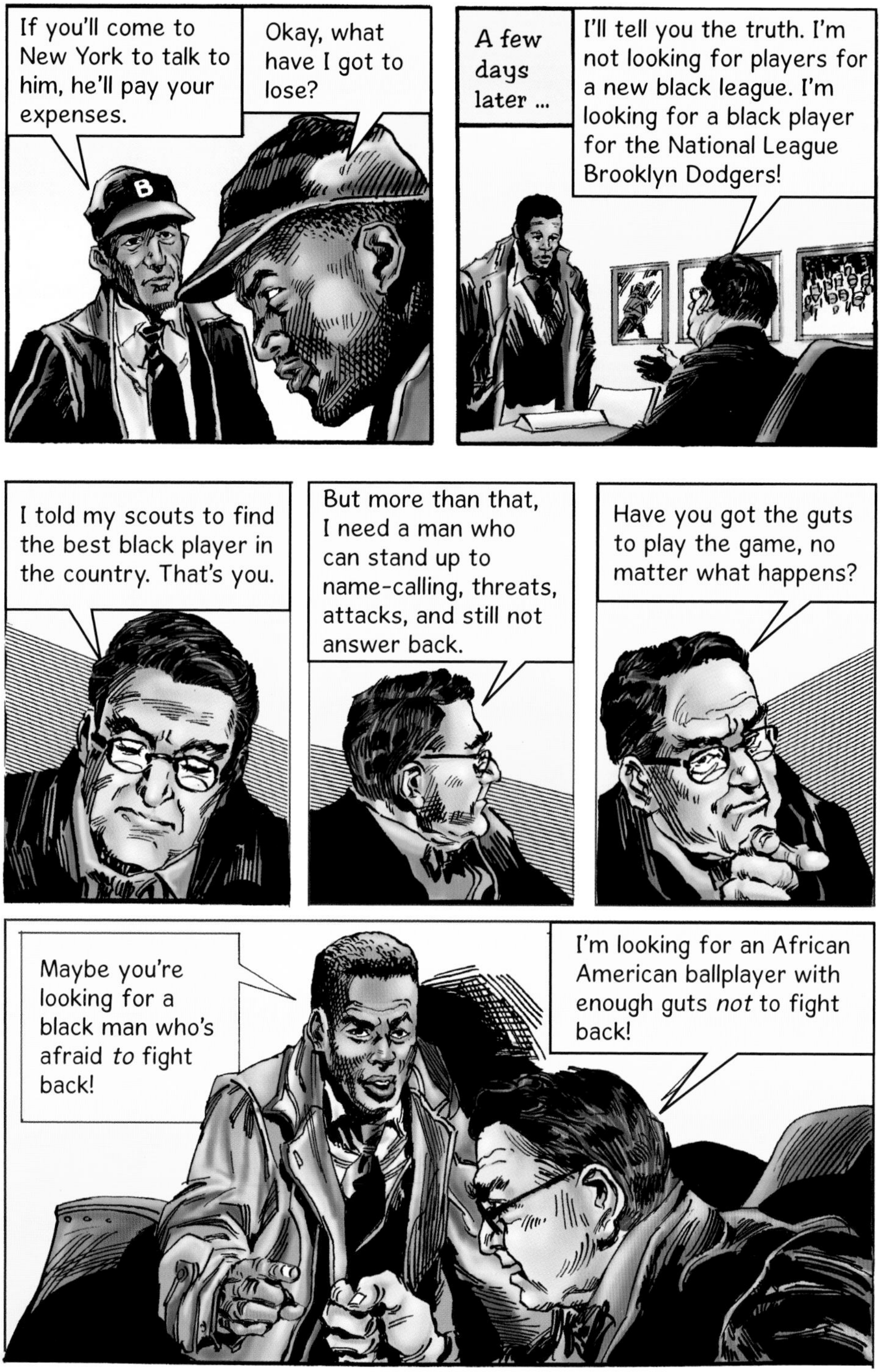
If you'll come to New York to talk to him, he'll pay your expenses.
Okay, what have I got to lose?
A few days later ...
I'll tell you the truth. I'm not looking for players for a new black league. I'm looking for a black player for the National League Brooklyn Dodgers!
I told my scouts to find the best black player in the country. That's you.
But more than that, I need a man who can stand up to name-calling, threats, attacks, and still not answer back.
Have you got the guts to play the game, no matter what happens?
Maybe you're looking for a black man who's afraid *to* fight back!
I'm looking for an African American ballplayer with enough guts *not* to fight back!

They talked for three hours. They became friends. Over and over Rickey warned Jackie of the troubles he would face. He agreed to play, starting at the Dodgers' farm club, the Montreal Royals.

Then ...

Now go call up your girl! There are times when a man needs a wife by his side!

On February 10, 1946, Jackie and Rachel were married.

Soon, they took a plane for spring training camp in Florida.

I'm a little scared going into the South for the first time!

I know California's not perfect, but at least there we could stand up for ourselves!

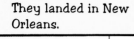
They landed in New Orleans.

You'll have to get off here— military priority.

But we have tickets to Daytona Beach!

After 12 hours, they flew on to Pensacola.

These seats are taken. You'll have to leave.

And how do we get to Daytona Beach?

They finished the trip riding for 16 hours in the back of a Jim Crow bus.

In spring training, things went well. But when they were scheduled to play a game in Jacksonville ...

We're supposed to play a game here this afternoon!

Game's called off. A city law says blacks and whites can't play together!

But the people in Montreal loved Jackie.

Yaaaaaaaaaaaay, Jackie!

He led the team in batting. They won their league pennant and then the Little World Series.

In November 1946, Jackie and Rae had a son.

Jack Robinson Jr.! Now I have more reason than ever to open up the major leagues to African Americans!

In January, Jackie was ordered to report for spring training in Cuba.

I'm to report to the Royals. The Dodgers are in Cuba too! I don't know for sure what Mr. Rickey plans.

And in Cuba ...

Practice with the Royals and learn to play first base! The Dodgers need a good first baseman.

I'll try ...

Concentrate ... hit that ball, get on base, steal, run wild, and play great baseball!

I'll do it!

Jackie followed orders.

What? That Robinson guy ... there he goes again!

I know, he's driving me nuts!

In seven Dodgers-Royals games, he batted .625 and stole seven bases.

Back in New York, on April 9, 1947, just before a game, press box reporters received a startling announcement.

Hey, read this! The Dodgers have signed Robinson!

It's happened! A black man's going to play in the major leagues!

Telegraph wires flashed the news to the sports' world. And Jackie went into a batting slump.

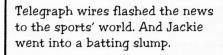

STRIKE THREE! You're out!

The team manager was Burt Shotton.

Twenty times at bat without a base hit! You oughta take me out of the lineup!

I know you can hit! Maybe you'll snap out of it in our next series with the Philadelphia Phillies.

The Phillies, led by their manager, started name-calling.

We don't want you here!

Go back to the cotton fields where you belong!

Jackie almost lost control.

He could imagine his fist smashing into a Phillies player.

Forget turning the other cheek. I'll fight back!

Then he thought of all Mr. Rickey had risked on him. So he lined the ball into center field for a hit.

It's a hit! Yaaaaaaaaaay, Jackie!

Since Jackie could not answer the insults, some of his teammates began to stand up for him.

You yellow-bellied cowards!

Many more balls were pitched directly at Jackie than at other players.

Every mail delivery was full of crank letters.

Threats to kidnap Jack Jr., to attack your wife, to kill you. I'm turning them over to the police.

But the Dodgers won the National League Pennant for the first time in six years; and a "Jackie Robinson Day" was held at Ebbets Field to honor him.

He has played in more games, scored more runs, hit safely more times, hit 12 home runs, and has led the team in stolen bases!

In 1949 a new day dawned for Jackie.

You've been a great ball player and a fine gentleman! Thanks to you there are five black players in the Majors and more on the way!

From now on, do what you feel like!

You mean pop off when I get mad like any other player? Great!

With the pressure removed, Jackie played better than ever.

ROBINSON LEADS DODGERS TO ANOTHER PENNANT

JACKIE ROBINSON NAMED MOST VALUABLE PLAYER

ROBINSON ELECTED TO ALL-STAR TEAM BY RECORD VOTE

In his ten years with the Dodgers, they won the Pennant six times, and the World Series once.

Jackie and Rae had two more children and moved to the house of their dreams in Stamford, Connecticut.

Come on, Jack! Strike him out!

After ten years with the Dodgers, Jackie retired from baseball and took a new job.

As you know, I'm the President of the Chock Full O'Nuts restaurant chain. We'd like to have you on our team, as Vice President.

If it's a real job, not just a publicity gimmick, I'd be interested!

**William Black**

We need you as personnel director. Most of our employees are African American. We have problems with turnover, absenteeism, and so on.

Good! I think I can do it!

Later, he talked with Roy Wilkins, head of the NAACP.

Jackie, will you head our Freedom Fund drive, a national effort to raise funds for our work?

I'd be proud to!

He traveled across country speaking about the work of the NAACP. The fund drive was a big success.

In 1956 he received the Spingarn medal from the NAACP.

This honor justifies my policy of speaking out whenever and wherever I've seen racial injustice.

In 1962 Jackie was elected to the Baseball Hall of Fame. He was the first black player ever eligible for the honor.

At the ceremony in Cooperstown ...

I want to share this moment with three people who have meant the most to me: my mother, my wife, and Mr. Branch Rickey!

That same year, Jackie wrote to Nelson Rockefeller, Governor of New York.

I am pointing out to the governor that not a single black has a top-level job or access to the governor to tell him of our concern and grievances.

As a result, Jackie met with Rockefeller. They worked together to bring about reforms.

Dr. Martin Luther King's Southern Christian Leadership Conference sponsored a dinner to honor Jackie.

We congratulate him on his career, and thank him for the work he has done for our organization.

Until the day in 1972 when a fatal heart attack struck him down, he never stopped working to correct injustice. People crowded the New York streets to watch his funeral procession.

There was never a more thrilling moment in baseball than watching Jackie Robinson steal home base!

The Reverend Jesse Jackson spoke.

This man turned stumbling blocks into stepping-stones and reminded us of our birthright to be free!

THE END